voice of the hive

VOICE
OF THE HIVE

ric masten

SUNFLOWER INK
Palo Colorado Road, Carmel, California. 93923

**CLACK &
NICHOLS**
A PARTNERSHIP

THE VOICE OF THE HIVE produced by Clack & Nichols,
A Partnership, 522 North Grant, Odessa, Texas 79761.
Telephone number (915) 337-8511.

Cover painting by Joe Dawkins

Illustrations by Max Karl Winkler

The songs are all published by MASTENSVILLE MUSIC
PUBLISHING, licensed through Broadcast Music, Inc.

(paperback) First printing 1978
          Second printing 1980
          Third printing 1983
          Fourth printing 1987

Library of Congress Catalogue Card No. 78-59786

ISBN 0-931104-02-5

for the poets in my life

i love what you do
to clean sheets
enough to kill
an electric blanket
and take on
the windmill
myself

Preface

There are those, afflicted with what Ric Masten calls "terminal cool," who tend to be wary of a sandy-bearded poet who goes traipsing all over occupied America in his old clothes, packing a 12-string guitar and 20 pounds of homemade poetry, reading and singing and talking with men, women and children in all kinds of situations. It can be unsettling. Poets are supposed to be shut up in anthologies, or at least shut up. Thus when Ric props his looseleaf life's work up on a music rack and begins with something like:

> "have you ever had someone coming
> you wanted to impress too much
> a guest who had you running
> to wash and scrub and straighten
> the place up
> until you could see clearly
> what an awful mess of squalor
> you really live in . . ."

Someone out in his audience may whisper to someone: "Who *is* this guy reading poems, anyway?" Who indeed. What kind of man would do a thing like that?

Oh, Walt Whitman, Carl Sandburg, Robert Frost, to mention a few. "Yes," the someone says, "but those guys are all in the Oxford book of humdingers." That's true, and isn't it lucky for us, since none of them are walking around anymore? It is equally lucky for us that since Ric's works are not yet available in the gold-embossed Hall of Fame edition, he *is* walking around, giving them to us first-hand.

But to the point. Where did he come from? Where is he going? And what is he doing here? He comes from California, where he was born in 1929, then spent a childhood clouded by his father's death, compulsory education and the overburden of his hovering mother.

Rebellion came early in his life and stayed on for the subsequent performance. After dropping out of five colleges in succession and noticing that he came away from every one still thirsting for knowledge, he grew to suspect that either he was a slow learner or life is full of ambiguities.

When the tide of social protest swelled in the early 1960s, Ric flung himself into it. He wrote poems, marched, sang, inveighed and became so infused with the heat and fervor of the new thought that when the radical tide subsided, killing many of its heroes in the sudden fall and scattering the rest into the limbo of the apathetic generation, he discovered that heat and fervor were two things he wasn't ready to do without. Though the marches were over, he kept walking, partly through momentum, partly because he had salted away enough lived experience to have strong feelings he wanted to express and others wanted to hear.

This is most visible in Ric's first volume of poetry. (Who's Wavin' 1970) Like hastily-packed suitcases, his early works reveal his basic philosophy of the affirmation and celebration of life, flung in beside polemics, politics and other souvenirs. Over the years and miles, he has learned to travel light.

When he met Robinson Jeffers near the end of the old poet's life, Jeffers told him: "Every artist has just one thing to say," and Ric says: "I already know and can tell you one phrase what my main statement is: 'You're not alone alone.' There are fringe areas out in left field, but in the end, if I write about how my mother is bugging me, what I want out of you is a response of 'Yeah! I'll be goddamned! Me, too!' And I think a poet's job, if he's about the business he should be, is to say things in such a way that you can recognize that that's what you always knew all the time."

Here, in Ric's sixth book, the pattern of his shots can be seen tightening around the bull's eye. the Voice of the Hive finds him somewhere near the halfway mark in a journey he intends to make a long and joyous one. If it is long, he will have satisfied himself that a soul which is carefully cleaned, oiled and regulated is good for greater mileage than the throw-away kind. If it is joyous, it will have justified his stubborn belief that there is hope for any world which manages to drag itself out of bed each morning, if only to lick its wounds.

Naturally a man who pursues ends such as these finds it necessary to take his own pulse a lot. If you discover that happening in these pages, don't waste time asking yourself if Ric is a hypochondriac. You may simply have reached the point at which you need to hear these works from the author's own lips in order to better appreciate his case history.

The above statement may seem presumptuous to those who prefer reading poetry to hearing it, but please believe no offense is intended. Battered as it is by the blows of the mass media, the language is in enough trouble without us getting into little quarrels of that kind.

Still it should be safe to say that owing to the need for a breakthrough in cloning technology which science hasn't yet made, the book's pages are simply a blueprint of Ric — the observations, the self-examination, the comparisons and the stated conclusions. It is in the flesh that he becomes a three-dimensional edifice in which the listener can see that no fretful hypochondriac behaves as Ric does — taking himself apart with the enthusiasm of a kid exploring a pocket watch. "Hey, wow!" you'll find him saying, "look at this big, long spring. And that funny thing swinging back and forth there." And what with all his waving and pointing, you're soon listening and smiling, standing beside him and peering down into a mess of internal workings, agreeing that these human beings are curious contraptions, and not only that, but noticing how your balance staff seems to work about the same way his does. It may even dawn on you then that if you don't get yourself wound up regularly, you won't keep ticking.

Even though that grade of experience usually comes across better in the telling than in the reading, don't throw this book away on that account. Ric has been drawing blueprints of lived experience for a lot of years, and he will get the message through to you, for he takes great pains not to clutter it with grandiose embroidery just for the sake of making the page look good. His written lines will jump up at you, saying: "This is what is happening, this is how I feel, this is what I see, this is how I know that we are all in this thing together."

Predictably, his gift for speaking simply and from the heart fosters dismay among those inclined to compile catalogues, those who in the interest of decorum would like to assign him an air-tight poetic job description. This tendency gets him variously labeled oral poet, folk philosopher, troubador, minstrel, even troubader-rhapsodist (mercy!). To that could be added meister-singer, jongleur, gleeman. But accurate as each term is in its own way, none quite captures the Ric Masten essense. Out of desperation and exhaustion one might surrender to the obvious and call him simply "poet".

Surely that is best. Ric Masten, poet. Walking around, refusing to industrialize, insisting on remaining a cottage industry, wearing his poems like shoes, sometimes well-polished, sometimes showing the scuff marks of a life lived at ground level where, careful as a person is, he can't always avoid stepping in something.

Along with its new poems, the *Voice of the Hive* contains several which old friends will recognize from an earlier work of Ric's entitled *Let It Be a Dance* (1975), now out of print. You will find them here once again but re-examined and given new luster, threaded into the lengthening necklace of Ric's story, which as all true stories must, keeps kaleidoscoping into new feelings in which old feelings are recognized as they come around full circle; felt again, as Ric feels them anew when he says:

> "there
> through it all
>   the voice of the hive
> calling us home"

There is an unavoidable element of folly in any written introduction to "an author and his works." If that author is himself writing on the same topic, then what need of an introduction, for who knows the material better than he? Since that is exactly what is happening here, this impossible task should be concluded so the reader may be led out of the wilderness of writing about writing and ushered on to the real green pastures.

But first this urging: If the living Ric Masten chances to walk your way, don't fail to let him tell you these poems in person. One of these days, he will be joining that remote little circle of humdingers on Parnassus. Meanwhile, he is ours.

Jack Kisling
Denver, Colorado
April 1978

Contents

THE AUTHOR

Author's Note

If the script for a play cannot come fully alive until it
has been staged then these bare bones of mine,
these "Speaking Poems" need the sound of a
human voice to flesh them out.

> Take this then
> in the spirit
> which it was given
> and speak to each other.

Part 1

FULL CIRCLE

A child is de—livered on the first day of spring in perfect condition an in-no-cent thing But as soon as you discover your fingers and toes You hide away your beauty up in———side your clothes. and you're taught what's wrong and you're taught what's right that you ought to know the difference in black and white it's called an ed-u-ca—tion and you'll get it til you're grown and after gradu-a-tion you'll be left all alone

Spring is green and the summer burns gold the autumn leaves fall the winter blows cold and the seasons they come and the seasons they go and the more I learn the less I know

child is de-livered on the first day of spring in perfect condition an innocent thing

a child is delivered
on the first day of spring
in perfect condition
an innocent thing
but soon as you discover
your fingers and toes
you hide away your beauty
inside your clothes

and you're taught what's wrong
taught what's right
that you oughta know the difference
in black and white
it's called an education
you get it till you're grown
then after graduation
you are left all alone

     spring is green
     summer burns gold
     autumn leaves fall
     winter grows cold
     the seasons they come
     the seasons they go
     and the more i learn
     the less i know

there's the question — the answer
and the space between
and summer is the season
to chase the dream
you're young enough to think
you're gonna win the race
you swear you'll never settle
for second place

but a dream gets stolen
and a dream gets lost
a stone stops rolling
and gathers moss
when you're getting the laughs
but not the joke
summer up and leaves you
at the end of your rope

Chorus

you begin to get the message
when you're forty or so
when the weather gets messy
an the autumn leaves blow
when you're not a bit closer
then you were before
you go to the window
on the forty-third floor

a life to live — a life to take
you decide to have another
slice of birthday cake
and tho you know you'll never win
you know you never could
you know you can't lose
if you can do it looking good

Chorus

winter comes to find you
feeling rich and wise
sixty years of going
through the lows and highs
and you want to share the wisdom
want to share the wealth
but you know enough to know
you gotta get it for yourself

so you carry on
till you loose your grip
till your mind gets feeble
and starts to slip
and when you get to acting
like a baby again
you'll go out
exactly
the way you came in

THE VOICE OF THE HIVE

when
the shadow of death
fell upon us
the queen mother died
and the swarm
        scattered
        far afield
social insects
self-aware now
        feeling utterly alone

        except
        in our dreams
        songs
        and poetry

there
through it all
the voice of the hive

calling us home

5

THE PRIESTS MOST HIGH

i have always thought
you had to go somewhere
to be in the presence of art
    to bare your head
    and keep your voice down

but this isn't art
art is a coffee cup
a pillow
a chair
the things we use
the things we wear
the shirt
the belt
the shoes
and it can be ugly
as a gas pump
or parking meter

what we hear in the music hall
see in the galleries
what poets say
and dancers do

    ah
    this is religion

THE ENLIGHTENED

when i was younger
i would shoot the rapids
on any subject
showboating in the shallows
and later on
enjoyed being in over my head
discussing the depth
of wider deeper places

however
having spent half my life
working both sides of this river
i feel i know the pools and eddies
fairly well
and when the conversation flows these days
i find it impossible
to wade right in

but don't misunderstand
this silence
for i do enjoy being here with you
listening
to the things you have to say

        and in some small way
        comprehending perhaps
        why the so-called enlightened
        simply stand
        by the water
        smiling
                        vacantly

THE DISAPPOINTED

did we arrive
like a shallow pleasure-seeking male
an ugly american abroad
terribly aware of ourselves
surveying the landscape
with a roving eye
looking for something to pick up
crudely violating your distant body
coming away
feeling cheated and unsatisfied
when you didn't produce
a single orgasm large or small

or did we appear
more like a nurturing female
the proverbial jewish mother
come to camp on the doorstep
of a close relative
uninvited
but full of good intentions
going home in a huff
feeling unwanted and rejected
when nothing there
would eat
our chicken soup

either way
we must be forgiven
it is a big universe
and no one
likes to sleep alone

THE CONSUMER

it is said that the buddha
turned back at the gate of nirvana
and is this not understandable
grasshopper
when you consider
how exhausting it would be
to spend even an hour as alive
                        and aware
as the people we see
on a 30-second TV spot commercial
can you imagine yourself being
that active
and effervescently involved
        with soda pop
        and irregularity

i am drained
at the very idea
of exerting the energy it would take
to soap my body that way

to even consider the possiblity
of being that glad and overjoyed
has given me a deep appreciation
of this drab
        empty
        lackluster life of mine
and i find
i have developed a real admiration
for anyone who has learned to live

        with a dingy smile
        and a swollen hemorrhoid

THE REALTOR

we pale faces
labor under a strange delusion
thinking that we beat the indians
out of manhattan island
    for a string of beads
    and a breakable promise
when in truth
they really shucked us out of our socks
we being dumb enough
to give up our valuables
    for a piece of real estate
when any fool knows
no one
can own the land

the problem was
that although we were gullible
    we were also stupid
and really believed the property was ours
and because of that innocent prank
those noble con men bit the dust
    horribly
i mean after all
was the loss of face
and some cheap jewelry
worth all that human carnage

but listen white eyes
    listen
    the red man's wisdom will prove out
twenty minutes
two thousand years
when the time is spent and behind you
what's the difference anyway

    in truth
    no one can own the land
    we can only care for it
        awhile

THE PRISONERS

though
i have seen the photographs
of those ragged
                weary men
still i think i envy them
the prisoners
captured in a good
                and holy war
which every war has been

caught and confined
by an obviously evil enemy
left to rot in some forgotten
prison camp
stubbornly clinging
                to secret information
for which i'd rather die
                than tell
surviving in a roach-
                and rat-infested cell
my eye fixed
on that thin sliver of hope
at the edge of the door
the crack of light
                that keeps us alive
in our solitary confinement

yes
there have been times
i've wished it were
                a simpler prison
for out here
in this open field of sunshine
it is far
        far more difficult
           to plan
                the great escape

THE ABORTED

1928 was a time!
a party i'm told
the last year of champagne
and confetti

and when the doctor said he
thought it was more than a hangover
she took up horseback riding
with a vengeance
jumped from the top
of the racquet club fence
and then eight months along
went to san francisco
with a back street address

i tell you this
before i go on to tell you
that the people who gave us

THE DEATH PENALTY

who produced those unforgettable scenes
like the governor of california
surrounded by a frenzy of women
who scream
        guillotine!
        guillotine!
                        those same people
are back promoting

THE FETUS

curling on the playbill page
like a crooked finger
like a question mark
like the end of 2001
asking me
        is your daughter
        guilty of MURDER?

enraged
i tell myself it's time
to come out against
this kind of obscenity

    then
    at the last possible moment
    mother changes her mind
    i'm saved again

and the tired old scenario
grinds to an end
where we find a man
not knowing what to say
resolve frozen in his hand
the pen
standing silent in the gantry

    mission aborted

THE RETARDED

songs
for raggedy anns and andys
assembled in the cafeteria
arranged around tables
a last supper frieze
the disciples propped up
in chromium chairs
a jumble of elbows and knees
and jesus was there
wearing a plastic white helmet
so that when falling down
he wouldn't hurt himself

frightened at first
i struck them a chord
gave them a beat to step on
which they did but not quite
putting their feet in the cracks
but it was all right
cause everyone laughed
and everyone grinned
and slather ran down an old man's chin
such waving of arms
and clapping of hands
i nearly broke down in
front of the fans
   they are very happy you know
   the retarded
   not the disturbed — the retarded
   when they are clean
   entertained and well-fed
   i have always found them
   quite content

we pay an awful price
to sit here quietly
hands folded
trying to understand something
as complicated as this

THE EXECUTIONER

he died, you know

oh god — i'm sorry
you hadn't heard
yes it's true
about a month ago

i must have killed alan watts
a thousand times
with a word

        oh god — i'm sorry
        you hadn't heard

and you my father
dead and gone all these years
receive a letter
from a long-lost boyhood friend
a letter which i will not answer
for a while

        enjoy
        enjoy

KITCHEN HELP

i keep this drawer in my life
        in my kitchen actually
where i put things like ironing cords
and green stamps and washers
and nuts and nails and pliers
screwdrivers and thumb tacks
        mousetraps and
balls of string unravelling
and small things i mean to fix one day
or had one too many of
        or lost the other half of
            or found and can't identify
and absolutely worthless
sentimental things

and i keep this pandora's box of mine
so jammed full of junk that it sticks
shut
and is impossible to open
without jerking the handle so hard
it comes out suddenly
. . . like a sick child
                vomiting
                on the floor
so i work at it slowly
first one side — then the other
grunting and straining
until its tangled interior is exposed
and even then
there's so much stuff to go through
i'm never really sure
i haven't missed
what i was looking for anyway

unlike god
        i bring forth very little
        from the chaos
and i wonder how many precious hours
        of my precious life i've wasted

16

brooding over that innocent face
closed
into the counter there
flagellating myself
for not taking a few minutes
to straighten it out
and file the contents
neatly away like laboratory specimens

IN CLEAN LABELED JARS

my roommate in boarding school did this
        we didn't hit it off though
        i found him rather dull
and he told me
i made him nervous

at times i think
i'll just dump the whole mess
into the garbage and be done with it
of course i never will
because
when i'm really searching for something
        desperately
it is most important to know
there is always
        at least one
                last place to look

AN ANTHROPOLOGIST

a young man
was caught trespassing
trying to steal the track
of a dinosaur

too bad
had he got away with it
he might have had it made
into a wall hanging
for all of us to see

and like an old anthropologist i met
living alone in schenectady
he would have had it
inscribed
     "and this too shall pass"

A JUMPER

not quite sure why i didn't buy
the hard rocky mattress
                    the super sleeper
i came back from my jumping-off place
and put it down
                    as a suicide poem

only to find
while rummaging around
for the punch line
                    birthday greetings

THE PHOTOGRAPHER

    i look so on top of it
        brow arched slightly
        eyes alive with good humor
        jaw set and yet around the mouth
        the hint of a smile
        all of the above
        below the illusion
        of a pile of hair

but damn — it bothers me
to see that face of mine
so full of confidence
gazing out
into the not-too-distant future
which is where i am today
doing my best
to recall that place in time

it was taken on request
that much i know and in a studio
so i'm sure the thing was posed
        clothes carefully chosen
        head tipped just so
        hair mussed as if by the wind
        lips moistened
        posture and expression
        set absolutely right

but like a suspicious dollar bill
i hold my glossy image to the light
and take a closer look
but still i cannot say if what i see
was real or not but if it was
then i fear
the hooded photographer took
more than my photograph that day

better to be caught
        with a finger in my nose

mouth wide open
eyes drooping closed
with a tree that seems
to be growing from my ear
appearing like an idiot
and yet
surrounded by those
who could love me still

if you must take my photograph — wait
till after the curtain calls are done
and catch me
falling off the stage into
the big bass drum

THE DEAF

imagine a woodsman
swinging an axe in the distance
the tree speaking out of sync
then nothing
except what is left in your eye
chips still fly
but your ears
dumb fleshy things
hang from your head
useless handles frozen stiff

the world around you
fills with dead air
the quiet thickens
till the atmosphere is packed solid
surrounding you like clear wax
and everyone there
rides in a limousine
stars of the silent screen
seen through shatterproof glass
the faces glide past
lips moving like goldfish

the trumpet has lost its voice
the seashell is mute as a dish

my god
in a place like this
what do you do with a word
like inconceivable?

spell it she said
hands moving behind the question
in a kind of semaphore
and you talk too fast

later that evening
the poems fell from my mouth
little naked birds
crying for life

and who would have known
they were there
had she not taken them into her care
holding them up
till they could fly on their own

and back where this began
the tree came crashing down
    and the sound
    was the sound
of the deaf
        applauding

A MAGICIAN

hey
how do you do that
    this
after my uncle jimmy
made a penny disappear
then smiling slyly found it again
in my ear

now to a seven-year old
this is the stuff of which
the meaning of life is made
and i begged him to reveal the mystery
and teach me to do it
and when he did i could see
                there wasn't much to it
except practice
and the fact that through it
i became the undisputed star
of the second grade
              which was all right
but making the magic
is never as much fun
as watching it made

we all love a magic show
and want to become a magician
and in a way we do
            each of us
developing a life style
creating an illusion
with a line of patter
            a trick or two
working within
a setting of our own design
getting good enough to spellbind
            at least a few
into catching their breath
as they enter our life saying:

hey how do you do this
                    and it works
                    for awhile
and it's fun for awhile
till the day you discover yourself
doing some sleight of hand
even you don't quite understand
and in order to be on top
of your own act
you take it apart
carefully
only to learn
that like the penny the loneliness
                    and anxiety
never really did vanish
it was just that during the performance
you forgot about it
but then knowing how to do the stunt
is not what keeps a real magician going
        what keeps him going
        has always been
                    the oooohs
                    and ahhhhs
and anyway would you really
want to walk around
                    with a penny in your ear?

AN ESCAPE ARTIST

if freedom is nothing more
than being able to choose your own cage
            as i suggest it is
then perhaps the fun comes
in being an escape artist

in recognizing the cage you are in
deciding how long you will settle for it
and then
when you want out
seeing how clever you are
at slipping through the wire

            perhaps the good life
                    the full life
            is nothing more
            than every once in a while
            pulling yourself through a hole
                    in the roof
            standing triumphantly
            looking down with a
                    hot damn
                        and then around
                            with an
                                oh shit!

AN ASTRONAUT

is it enough
to be the attendant pumping gas
into a car driven by someone who works
the night shift
at a factory making parts
for one small component
in a rocket engine?

    no
    not when you want to fly

so let's have another space shot
only this time
not a carefully picked highly trained
physically fit super intelligent
astronaut
this time
chosen by national lottery
an unqualified overweight
over forty beer drinking
sports fan like me
someone who still doesn't know
how they go to the john up there

what a moment it would be
the world watching
as i'm stuffed into a silver suit
strapped onto a capsule couch
slapped on the helmet
bolted in
counted down
and blasted off
sent up into the night
into the stars
out — so far
i'd give anything to be back
where i am
right now

THE SENILE

a child
does not watch a frog leap
a child is
a frog leaping
into the street
   oblivious
   indestructible
and later
much later
exactly like this
grandfather
a child again
off to meet the wizard
   meets the end
a kindly truck
coming swiftly
with a good night

 (kiss)

and may i be as lucky

THE DECEASED

he left
but not with someone
he'd made coffee for

      not with someone
who ironed his shirts
and scrubbed out his drawers

nor was he on the road
toward an illusion of something better

      his death
      was not tragic
      only the circumstance
      that surrounded it

on my dying day
      let me be loved
            loving
                  on my way

A MINISTER

he rode a pale white horse — away
he was twenty six
    O.D.'d
    killed himself with heroin
and although i didn't know him
i am a minister
    so i said this
    at his memorial service

first
i said his name
and then i said that he was old enough to say
i am
    and so he was
the proof of it gathered before me
    in them
who had known him first hand
    in them
who were more than they might have been
    because of his being

again i said his name
    and then i said
that even i who had never met him
    had met him there
    in them that day

a pebble does not
enter a pond without
    a
    ripple
    moving out
    and in time touching
every single shore — we are all
every one of us in this thing together

    again i said his name
and then i said that he had been
this was certain

and he having been must always be

      nothing is lost
      nothing is wasted
      no one
      none of us
      not one of us
      is that
          alone

RAINBOW'S END

It was just a run-down truck stop a greasy spoon ca·fe
twenty years be hind me now seems like yes ter day I was
on my way to somewhere to pull off some big deal
like every kid of twenty the in-ventor of the wheel I had
scrambled eggs and coffee a piece of buttered toast and the
drivers at the counter were more talkative than most
and when the subject wasn't women they talked about the road and the
miles that they had traveled and the weight of the load
Funny ain't it funny how it all comes 'round again it was just a run-down
truck stop and they called it Rain —————— bow's End.

it was just a run-down truck stop
a greasy spoon cafe
twenty years behind me now
seems like yesterday
i was on my way to somewhere
to pull off some big deal
like every kid of twenty
the inventor of the wheel

i had scrambled eggs and coffee
a piece of buttered toast
and the drivers at the counter
were more talkative than most

        and when the subject wasn't women
        they talked about the road
        and the miles
        that they had traveled
        and the weight of the load
        funny — ain't it funny
        how it all comes round again
        it was just a run-down truck stop
        and they called it rainbow's end

and i sat there feeling empty
as those poor devils spoke
if that was all there was to life
then it's a short length of rope
but remember i was twenty
i've covered ground since then
i've picked up on philosophy
and call a greek my friend

i've looked into religion
read sartre and camus
i've been up on the mountain
with an old guru

and when the subject wasn't women
we talked about the road
and the miles
that we had traveled
and the weight of the load

funny
ain't it funny
how it all comes round again
it was just a run-down truck stop
and they called it rainbow

zen

Part 2

NOTICE ME

Put me in your hum an eye come taste the bit-ter
tears that I cry Touch me with your human hand
hear me with your ear but notice me
damn you notice me I'm here
we can't be bothered now the
distant voices said when I'd come to share the butter—fly I
found and I would look up in—to the
nos trils of the fac es over — head and I never caught the
giants lookin down
ending
Notice me I am

put me in your human eye
come taste the bitter tears that i cry
touch me with your human hand
hear me with your ear
but notice me!
damn you — notice me!
                     i'm here

we can't be bothered now
the distant voices said
when i came to share
the butterfly i found
and i'd look up into the nostrils
of the faces overhead
but i never caught the giants
lookin' down

Chorus

yeah, i'm the poor misshapen figure
in the backroom of your home
your little baby's gone
and blown his mind
he's at the nursery window
standin' all alone
trying to catch the eye
of the blind

put me in your human eye
come taste the bitter tears that i cry
touch me with your human hand
hear me with your ear
but notice me
damn you — notice me!
                     i am

AN INDIVIDUALIST

there is a whole world of insects
            working in the garden
each one doing exactly
what he is expected to do
            and it bugs me
that the pollsters
can predict human behavior
as accurately and as easily
as if we were a bunch of aphids

the fact that they can tell
to a decimal point
how many of us will be there
and what we will do there
seems to me so undignified
            and degrading
that for awhile there
i'd find out what the polls were saying
and then got out and do
just the opposite
            strike a blow for freedom
            as it were
that was until i found out
they have statistics
on this sort of behavior also

so i'm left with nothing to do
but stir mustard into my coffee
and wonder
how many of us come next election day
are gonna go down and run
            naked
through a post office

            striving to be singular
            and unique
            if i succeed
i suppose they will put me away
with all the other crazies

THE INNOCENT

                              i have always been
one of those poor guilt-ridden souls
who automatically let up on the gas
when i pass the highway patrol
convinced that they'll get me
for what? i don't know
till they pull me over
and give me a ticket for driving too slow

years of nervously living
in the rear-view mirror
i finally decided to take it to court
where i sat and i waited till the jury
filed in with averted eyes
they always appear this way
feeling guilty themselves
if that's what they found you
or too cool to flash the A-OK sign around
and i was relieved when the verdict came
down
            not guilty
                        relieved not surprised
for i've had a battery of shrinks
on my side working night and day
persuading themselves
that i personally
            am not to blame
            for the orphaned
            the sick
            the hungry and lame

not guilty
            even i was convinced
by the brilliant defense that was built
and today i can say
that i only feel guilty
when i'm not feeling
                        guilt

A TAR BABY

she waits in the brier patch
         sweet as honey
         tacky as tar
in her thorny ambushes she waits
and practices her guitar and her
         i don't know
         what you're talking about
song and dance
         till i come along
         her half-witted son
she'd say
         and i would agree
for anyone with a lick of sense
knows enough to leave a tar baby be

still
through much perseverance
                  i've learned
ways
to handle the whole messy business
of the child/parent relationship
         and can do it these days
         with a certain dispatch
                  and expertise

the safest approach is
         to stay out of reach
and when least expected sneak up
         on the snare and yell
                  tar baby
                  i love you
then run like hell
sometimes i can be two blocks away
before she knew i was there

or if you're a glutton for punishment
you can survive keeping in mind
the fact that you deal
with something as primal as

the la brea tar pit
a quagmire of glutinous stuff
that sucked up
and gummed up
the fearsome tyrannosaurus
but these being civilized times
if it seems important enough
go ahead pay the tar baby a call
do it
put yourself through it
maybe twice a year
but that's all
however
never stand outside that door
thinking you know what it's all about
thinking
this time i'm going in there
and i'm gonna straighten
the tar baby out
oh yes
let me say this in closing
my oldest daughter
has turned twenty-two
and someone is coming
br'er rabbit
is that you

PARENTS

unopened as yet
the envelope turns in my hand
and
i suppose the flying wallendas can
but i never could stand at ease
watching my children
 play in the woods
 play in the trees
so certain was i that they would fall
and they did
and they didn't

but now that they have grown old
as i was then
out on their own
sending messages home
 as to where they are
 and how they've been
the envelope turns in my hand
and nothing has changed at all

THE FAN

you ask
do i know joan baez
well let me count the ways

    it was the summer of '67
    in the afterglow
    of a big sur celebration

    she was barefoot
    and wore a blue velvet gown
    her presence filled the room
    and children
    followed her around

    we had a friend in common
    who brought us together
    laughing as we joggled cups
    from one hand to the other

    her touch was firm and cool

    and though a hundred years go by
    i'll not forget
    what joanie had to say
    the day
    we held each other
    in each other's eye

    "hi"

or are you really asking
does joan baez know
she knows me

A FRIEND

if you're like me
even though
you're not quite sure of the question
you keep looking
for the answer
and every now and then you bump into
someone who's looking good
looking wise
so you tag along behind 'im
picking up the punch lines
thinking
hot damn
this one's gonna get me home free

and if you're like me
you go along with 'im
'til they say something stupid
do something human
and the whole thing
goes off the edge of the table
and shatters like a lamp

sometimes
when it matters enough
you try to put it back together
and what you come up with
is far from perfect
but a whole lot easier to live with

and then if you're like me
you go out
looking again

THE UNFAITHFUL

sleep!
recently
i have been going to you
as an old fool to a secret lover
and not unlike a tired salesman
bored with his territory
i have been giving into temptation
sneaking off in the afternoon
for a quickie little nap
a diversion
always coming out of it
with a start
a twinge of fear
telling myself
i shouldn't be here like this with you

but late in the evening
when the time is right
and what we do together
is socially acceptable
shamelessly
i can give myself to you completely
        forgetting the past
        letting the future go

and oh
how i hate to leave you in the morning

sleep!
you have become an acceptable death

            lovers of life
            — a warning —

THE PROJECTIONIST

*(When the creative urge has no place
to go, it backs up and under pressure
is transformed into anxiety.)*

it happens like this
i being a salesman of sorts
am out on the road
peddling rhyme and a theory of time
to other men's sons while mine back home
falls in among those
who deal in junk and
    steal and
    have dirty fingernails
    you know the type
then at the wheel of a car he swiped
the inevitable chase
the hair-raising ride
    to the killing ground
where like bonnie and clyde
he's brought down by the law
    to die in the dust
    of a backwoods road
    screaming the name of his pa
while i'm on stage in milwaukee
receiving your gracious applause

    you know i ought to become
    a suspense and horror movie producer
    spending as much time as i do
    in the projection booth
    scaring myself to death
    with my own warped imagination
    in bed before it's time to get up
    is when i do my best work
    using that gray
        empty space
to screen the rushes
of plot possibilities
cranking out sordid little gems like:

because a vegetarian told her
not to put chemicals into her body
my scatterbrained daughter
        goes off the pill
        gets pregnant
and then three months along
ill with german measles
too proud to phone us and ask for help
she runs off to wander
the cold
        hard streets of the city
alone and penniless
selling her blood for money
        to pay the abortionist fee
while i'm away in new england
making poems under a tree

or maybe i see myself
so involved in my work
        my wife starved for affection
goes out and joins an encounter group
having a real gut experience
and shortly thereafter runs off
with the leader a
        kissy
        huggy
        long-haird creep
who wears a mexican sarape
and a five-pound ankh around his neck
using the group grope technique
to recruit good christian women
to come work
in his san francisco massage parlor

and sometimes when i really get going
i can follow the story line
clear to the end
where the music swells
and i see myself old
        and tired
        and feeble

47

dying in the men's room
of a greyhound bus station
a ticket to pocatello idaho in my hand

now everyone knows
it takes a certain amount of
        drama
        suspense
        and tragedy
to keep life interesting
but this is ridiculous

THE TOP SEEDED

he perfected his service
his opening statement
until it could not be returned

he entered many conversations
but he died alone

center court
in his spotless whites

THE BEAUTIFUL

wherever she went
in that crowded
     chattering room
the conversation dimmed
as if something were wrong
with the electricity

she was that beautiful
the men running their eyes over her
like hands
the women bunching up
     into small clenched fists
     shouting at each other
     about babies
     and pregnancy

the poet in me must have been showing
because she came over
     and leaned close
     with an unlit cigarette
and as i fumbled for a light
she said
quite confidentially

     it's like i had a goiter

A TIME STEPPER

i couldn't help but note
that she was the only one in the room
up and dancing
    doing the tango
she explained
she'd always been a time stepper
    stepping forward stepping back
stopping through only long enough
    to repaint the bedroom
    the usual blue
a quality she had always been partial to
and he coming in from the office
where he really lived and died
surprised by her dropcloth and bucket
enough to speak his mind
for the first time
in a twenty-nine year old marriage
told how much he despised her
    cobalt
    turquoise
    vicks bottle
    point of view
and she
mourned for a week
not over what he had said
but because she just realized
she'd been sleeping alone
for twenty-nine years
and had never known
    never knew
but he's gone now
dead
she said
sweeping into a deep dip
holding tight to an illusion
    we all do
they will tell you it takes two to tango
but it just ain't so
    it just ain't true

THE RUNAWAYS

i as a bystander — as a spectator
would have to admit
they made it an extremely human race
but the villain
      mortgage in hand
          kept pace
a tireless runner
his footfall
      just a step or two behind
his shadow
a reminder on the ground

      chased them all the way
      to oregon — he did
      and caught them at the tape
oh—
they got to paradise
alright
but simply found another place
          like utah

A LOSER

these last eighteen days
we have rubbed our eyes raw
on a mile-high plume of smoke
while the marble cone fire
darkened the face of august
and stopped the sun down
till it seemed twice its size
washing our life and times
with a dim amber light

it looks like the end of the world
we said
as if we had some kind
of genetic foresight

THE DAMAGE ASSESSMENT

175,000 acres burned.
272 sq. miles of watershed gone.
A recreation resource lost.
The cost, in human terms:
Fourteen million dollars.

but the wilderness has lost nothing
it lives and breathes
in another time frame
even now
deep beneath the embers
tomorrow is moving

there is more than one
cathedral of trees
in the los padres rocks

but not for me
not for me

THE SURVIVORS

sometimes
i let the everyday mail
the bills and propositions
push me to a place
where i would welcome
a calamity of nature

a wildfire
out of control
raging through
the piles of collected junk
i can't get rid of
razing all that i have
except the opportunity
to begin again

perhaps
a catastrophic flood
sweeping away
a life that has become
a complicated nuisance
leaving behind an acre
of straightforward mud and muck
to deal with

or best of all an earthquake
shaking me out
of this unreasonable depression
a seismic upheaval
large enough
to level everything
and replace it
with something real
to dig out from under

all of us
left in the aftermath
with coffee in a paper cup
talking it over around
a red cross truck

how awful
how wonderful

along the san andreas fault
you'd be surprised
how many there are
secretly hoping

GYPSIES

Esalen

on highway one
caravans continue to and from esalen
everyone it seems
is on some kind of road these days
dominating conversations
with fine sounding directions
          found in current
          religious and philosophic
          road maps
rolling from guru to guru we go
like gypsies
searching not for a home
but a space to park the wagons for a night
    a place to steal a chicken
         or two
         from

i doubt if anyone really wants
to change his way of life
though
all of us i'm sure
would like to know
how to make the scary feelings go
            away

THE TRANSACTUALIZED

i have found
that other people's
odors
offend me
much more than my own

but the salad dressing
always tastes better
in your house

THE HOST & HOSTESS

have you ever had someone coming
you wanted to impress too much
a guest who had you running
to wash and scrub and straighten
the place up
until you could see clearly
what an awful mess of squalor
you really live in
   someone coming
who had you aware of spotted rugs
and torn upholstery
and dishes that were chipped
and didn't match—scratched tables
   someone coming
who had you angry at the kids
for ancient crayon marks
and beebee holes
who had you out pickin' up a yard
that could have been a garden
cursing weeds
that should have been a lawn
   someone coming
who had you hating yourself
and that cramped ugly little kitchen
where your weeping sullen wife
is banging pots and pans around
burning a tasteless dinner
that will go with the cheap wine
she says
her cheap husband bought

have you ever let someone
who hadn't even arrived yet
rob you of all your magic
and then later in the evening
had a sunset happen
that made you feel ashamed?

well that makes two of us

THE NOUVEAU RURAL

it's why we live here
terry said

this last 4th of july
when we awoke to a water tower
drained dry
useless faucets
and a mile and a half of empty PVC
the mountainside went wild
    waving wrenches
    running beside the pipe
    bumping into each other
    Mack Sennett
    looking for leaks in the line
and for awhile
till the toilets flushed again
    at least
there was meaning
and direction
    in the lives
    of eight
    middle-aged men

THE JUGGLER

it began with oranges
two at first then more
things naturally swarmed in his hands
and at the grocery store
where he worked as a young man
his head was the sun
and the planets
                    an egg
                    a bottle of ketchup
                    a box of cornflakes
                    a jar of jam
and once
when the manager wasn't looking
                    an eight
                    and a half pound
                    leg of lamb
the bag boys were impressed
and he obsessed now
with his own dexterity
threw in
                    a can of soup
                    a sack of flower
                    a quart of milk
keeping it up
until he had an entire grocery list
in orbit
under control
then to the imagined drum roll
he would add
                    the single
                    pringle potato chip
wow!

and over the years
he was not taken out
by the temptation
of adding one too many
                    brussel sprouts

and even
when his body was so on top
of this juggling act
that his mind had time
to step aside and ask him
why he was keeping
all that garbage up in the air
he held fast
in the face of that kind of self-doubt

he was good all right
really good
but he didn't become great
till the night
he dropped everything
except the
                              oranges

which he sat down and ate

THE HUNCHBACK

up there
you are a prince among gargoyles
and by comparison
i would seem misshapen

but in another chorus line
there are things
quasimodo
that could get in the way
of any real communication

    deformities
    not yours
    mine
you see i have this odd
twisted nature
that cannot pretend you don't
    walk funny
    when you do
that will not ignore the fact
that your coat doesn't quite fit
or that your left eye
    has slipped a bit

and if you are unwilling
to suffer through the hells
of my disability
which is the desperate need
to talk to you about yours
then we can never give each other
more than the time of day

with me quasimodo
there is only one way to the tower
to the place
where we can ride the bells

    together

THE LOVER

in the eye of the end
                    i am dancing
on the moments that surface
like stepping stones
                    crossing over
i keep waving you out of sight
but somewhere else
is nailed to the wall
                    secure
                    immobile
                    and safe

who courts pain and freedom
these days
        not many

        for they come together
like hands
reaching out
for the electric touch
                    the ZAP!

and i have found it is the space
between the fingers
where close
is at

I, THE CATERPILLAR

I the cater pill-lar did see saint but-ter

fly I was workin at my weavin' and I saw her flutter

by and I wondered that a thing could be so fragile and so

frail dancin' on the li — lacs

all the way to jail And I hung her in a

pale white cage up in a broken tree and I longed to climb in-

side her eyes and listen to the sea and I would give my

bo-dy to be lifted by her wings but I the cat-ter

pil lar am tangled in my strings

I the cat ter pil lar and St. Butter-fly

i the caterpillar
did see saint butterfly
i was working at my weaving
and i saw her flutter by
and i wondered that a thing
could be so fragile and so frail
dancing on the lilacs
all the way to jail

and i hung her
in a pale white cage
up in a broken tree
and i longed to climb inside her eyes
and listen to the sea
and i would give my body to be lifted
by her wings
but i the caterpillar
am tangled in my strings

for who
would have the grocer
check the items from the list
and when my loves are sleeping
there are eyelids to be kissed
and the yellow bus keeps coming
at four o'clock each day
and i the caterpillar
cannot get away

and if i had a pair of wings
and knew i wouldn't fall
then the simple act of flying
it don't mean much at all
and if i jumped without them
well i wonder what we'd find
in all the empty rooms
i would go and leave behind

so i the caterpillar
will keep working at my trade

and i won't know what i'm weaving
until i get it made
if i don't believe in butterflies
i can tell you this
we all will do what we must do
simply to exist

                    i, the caterpillar
                    and saint butterfly

the Author

HOMESICK SNAIL

Have you ever heard the story 'bout the home — sick snail?
You'll find him in the garden at the end of a tear—stained trail
the ant is in his anthill and the bug be—neath a stone
but the snail slips down that winding road
trying to find his home
Home — sick slid-in' a long
feeling home—sick but where does a
home — sick snail be—long?

(Childrens song)

did you ever hear the story
of the homesick snail
you'll find him in the garden
at the end of a tearstained trail
the ant is in his anthill
the bug beneath a stone
but the snail slips down
that winding road
tryin' to find his home

homesick
slidin' along
feelin' homesick
but where
does a homesick snail belong

the spider is contented
in her spider web
the butterfly right at home
flyin' overhead
and deep within the woodwork
the termite drills a hall
and each and every cricket
has his hole in the wall

Chorus

the fuzzy caterpillar
is asleep in his cocoon
the angleworm digs underground
where there's lots of room
the centipede and beetle
each have found a place
but the homesick snail
goes racing round at a snail's pace

Chorus

i guess he's born to wander
yes i guess that's all he knows
cause everytime the snail arrives
he thinks it's time to go
sliding down that highway
down that silver track
searching for the very thing
he carries on his back

Chorus

we all live in the garden
and i am the snail

HANDS

i think of my poems and songs
as hands
and if i don't hold them out to you
i find i won't be touched

if i keep them
in my pocket
i would never get to see you
seeing me
seeing you

and though i know from experience
many of you
for a myriad of reasons
will laugh
and spit
and walk away unmoved
still
to meet those of you
who do reach out
is well worth the risk
                    and pain

so
here are my hands
do what you will

71

WRITER'S CRAMP

lately i've been caught
in a period of poetic irregularity
each day
like a good boy
i sit down at a prescribed time
to do my duty
and that's it
i just sit
trying to force a line

stuck behind locked doors
bearing down for hours
and nothing moving
except the patterns in the tile
where i stare at the floor

what's a body to do
when the rhymes don't come through
there must be something
a poet could be privy to
some trick of nature

     like prunes
     or castor oil

i've been told a sudden calamity
can be cathartic
that you can have the verses
scared out of you
i know a friend
and a bottle of wine
can loosen things up
but believe me it's no fun
knowing ya got one in there
and you can't get it out

maybe i'm pregnant
maybe having a poem
is like having a baby
they come

when they're ready
little creatures
howling into our lives
with a mind of their own

in any event
it's not happening here
and i've reached the point in this
where it's obvious
i need either
        a mild laxative
        or a natural disaster

THE LETTER T

to begin with
the idea of building a house
    all by yourself
is a stifling thought
with more than enough mystery
        beneath the floor
        and hidden in the walls
to frighten most laymen
into forgetting
you can only drive one
                    nail
                    at a
                    t
                    i
                    m
                    e
and even a journeyman
who thinks too much
about the pile of wood facing him
becomes lethargic
obsessed with the thought of
        five o'clock
which makes him a suicide

and maybe this is why
i run for boards during coffee break
keeping in mind
the fact
that the letter
t
is on the business end
of the key
i should punch up
nex

THIS DUSTY RUG

i hate it here writing
and wonder
what kind of masochism
drives a man
to try to pound
some sense out of a grinning
little machine
and stretch these painfully thin lines
for tightrope walkers
to play on
just over the hill
now where's the fun in that?

or in locking one's self up each day
to shout words
that fly against the glass
like confused birds
looking for the open sky

    yet stupidly
i hammer away
at this dusty rug
hoping to wind up
with something clean
and reveal a design
    more than one
can recognize
working in a cloud
of my own making
i try to remember
what it felt like
the last time
the bridge held
knowing full well
it can't be remembered
only experienced

VEG-O-MATIC

your body speaks to my cynic
    skeptic
slouching down there folding the arms
protecting the vitals
from what must be some new kind of
    old shell game
well squint those watchful eyes
lone ranger
and sit there behind your hand
    your mask
and bite your silver bullet and forget
the wisdom of that simple indian
on your color set
for what you see is what you get

as for me it's been nine years in a row
i have gone down front
    and stood slack-jawed
before one of the great men of our time
the guy who demonstrates and sells you
the vegetable slicer
at the county fair

now i know that thing is not gonna cut
a potato for me like it does for him
whomp! . . . french fries
with an attachment that carves radishes
into christmas trees
i know when i get that thing home
it's just gonna take the end of my thumb off
for me it don't slice tomatoes
it smashes 'em
    but i have bought
    nine of those things
    nine years in a row

so who's buying a vegetable slicer
i can tell a worthless piece of junk
when i see one

i'm simply paying the man a paltry sum
for giving me a few truly golden moments
trying to be like a kid i once knew
who was free
                    free to enjoy
almost everything
because you know
he really didn't care
if he was a sucker
                    or not

THE TEACHER ALONE

i suppose anyone fat-headed enough
to stand up in front of more
than one person and try to say something
                    deserves what he gets

but if you're being rude
because you've spent so much time
with your televison set

ignoring walter cronkite
and/or
beating your toy on the floor
in front of captain kangaroo
that you've gone and lost sight
of reality
then i must respond
and call you on it

if i don't
and just let it slide
i might as well be on TV
and this room really is twenty-four inches
wide
and absolutely empty

TO COUGH

to cough — according to webster
is to expell air suddenly and
noisily from the lungs through
the narrow opening between the
vocal cords and the larnyx, this
as a result of an involuntary
muscular spasm in the throat

it happens most often at poetry readings
music recitals
and/or other dignified public events

there are coughers and coughees

the cougher (usually singular)
is the one who engages in this activity
the one who struggles to keep the mouth
clamped over the sound while desperately
looking around for an easy way
out of the room

the coughees (usually plural)
are the ones who bend forward pretending
that nothing is happening
but whose interest
has left the front of the room and is now
down in a pocket wondering
if that stray lozenge
is still in there somewhere
but even if it is
it will have gathered so much lint
as to be an embarrassment
and like a teenage son with too much hair
go unintroduced
and all of the above is happening
while pablo casals gallantly
tries to play cello in a kennel
and it is such a truly human moment

it is beautiful

OLD ROBERT FROST

i saw old robert frost
in pasadena last fall
he stumbled around
in a celluloid dream
that somebody caught and kept
old robert frost
stirring his milk with a spoon
till it spilled
and i said to myself
      why you crafty old buffoon

in one of his lighter moments
he remarked with a wink
      that you can't write a poem
      to pay a bill
      that's not what they're for

so i think i'll extend
that thought
this much more
having nothing else in the bank
no savings at all
except
old robert frost
and a wolf at the door

THE BEGGAR

anything but blind
he sat a long time
pretending not to see

and then
he set his volumes out before him
like pencils
and slowly got to his feet

there is nothing quite as sad
as the sight of an old poet
tap dancing in the hall
outside the office
of student affairs

A PERFECT POEM

couple of poets talking
stringing sentences together
stretching lines
hanging words out in the wind
speaking sheets and pillowcases

and in between the flap and billow
of our voices
fluttering down before us
    a
    pale
    blue
    feather
        fallen
        from some passing bird

HANDS #2

i have these hands

the right one
swings the hammer
        building

the left
holds the nail
        and dreams
they
work together

THINK OF ME
as music

Wake me in the morning   Take me to the plane

yester day is over now   to morrow never came

It's time to get the guitar down   and hit the friendly skies

Time to have a—nother round of hellos   and good bys   Well I

Gonna taxi down that   runway   turna - round to

go   and as we climb   and circle

I'll look for you be - low   and somewhere in the future

a - lone with my guitar   I'll sing for

you   this song for you   and you know   who you are

wake me in the morning
take me to the plane
yesterday is over now
tomorrow never came
it's time to get the guitar down
and hit the friendly skies
time to have another round
of hellos and good-byes

i guess i let my coffee
sit there getting cold
i really didn't want it tho
just something warm to hold
while i look at you and wonder
why a good thing has to end
and if i'll ever pass this way
and be with you again

gonna taxi down that runway
turn around to go
and as we climb and circle
i'll look for you below
and somewhere in the future
alone with my guitar
i'll sing for you
this song for you
and you know who you are

so think of me as music
think of me as rhyme
and if you ever need a friend
just bring me to your mind
but like a melody i gotta be
free to drift along
so i think i'm gonna change my name
and call myself a song

in forty-seven minutes
they're gonna put that big bird down
and i'll step into an airport

and play another town
meet another stranger
make another friend
share a song
get it on
and then be gone again

so think of me as music
think of me as rhyme
and if you ever need some love
just bring me to your mind
but like a melody
i've just got to be
free to sail along
so i think i'm gonna change my name
and call myself a song

PAST THIS POINT

words
    stand
        out
           dark
               stiff
                  pickets
on a page
    white
    and silent
    as a snowfield
the plow moves along
beside the fence
like a finger
and uncovers a road
    words
    indicate
    direction
    only
all else
is found between the lines
and beyond the period
at the end of the sentence
past this point
        the living
        and dying
        really goes on